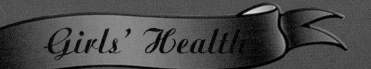
Girls' Health

Dealing
with PMS

Sophie Waters

rosen publishing's
rosen
central®

New York

Published in 2008 by The Rosen Publishing Group, Inc.
29 East 21st Street, New York, NY 10010

Copyright © 2008 by The Rosen Publishing Group, Inc.

First Edition

Library of Congress Cataloging-in-Publication Data

Waters, Sophie.
Dealing with PMS / Sophie Waters.—1st ed.
     p. cm.—(Girls' health)
Includes bibliographical references and index.
ISBN-13: 978-1-4042-1949-6
ISBN-10: 1-4042-1949-8
1. Premenstrual syndrome—Juvenile literature.
I. Title. II. Title: Dealing with premenstrual syndrome.
RG165.W38 2008
618.1'72—dc22

                                                    2007013197

Manufactured in the United States of America

Contents

Introduction

Premenstrual syndrome (PMS) is a term used to describe a group of symptoms some women experience between two weeks and three days before their menstrual period. Although many women report various symptoms and kinds of discomfort, the most common complaints are a bloated feeling, mood changes, food cravings (such as for salty or sweet foods), headaches, and backaches. The symptoms of PMS can come back every month and around the same time every month.

Because of their discomfort, some young women with PMS miss school or work. These women may not be able to do the things they are used to doing. If you suffer from PMS, you may feel like your life is repeatedly disrupted. It may seem unfair if you are unable to do the things you are used to doing. This might leave you feeling depressed, frustrated, or angry. However, there are things you can do to alleviate your symptoms of PMS. The first step toward dealing with your PMS, however, is to understand more about it.

1

Your Body Inside and Outside

To understand premenstrual syndrome (PMS), it is important to know about your body and the changes it experiences.

Puberty

Puberty is a time of rapid physical change in young men and women. For females, in addition to growth, you will experience the following changes:

- Your breasts grow.
- Your sweat begins to have a strong odor (often called B.O., or body odor).
- You get more fatty tissue around your hips, thighs, and buttocks.

Sometimes the physical and emotional changes that come with puberty can be confusing or seem overwhelming.

- Hair grows on your armpits, between your legs, and more heavily on your legs.
- Your skin and hair become oily.
- Your menstrual period begins.

Puberty is also a time of emotional changes. Often you can't seem to control what happens to your mood. You can, however, learn ways to control your behavior and how you deal with your reactions. Knowing that the changes in your body and your emotions are normal can be comforting. Finding someone to talk with, such as a good friend or a trusted adult, will help, too.

Hormones

Hormones are chemical substances that are made by organs in your body and circulate in your blood. Your body makes hundreds of hormones, and they are responsible for many of

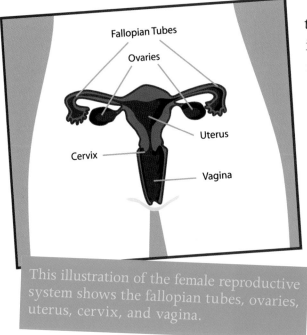

the changes that happen in your body. They are made in particular organs and cause changes in other parts of your body. Hormones cause the start of menstrual periods.

This illustration of the female reproductive system shows the fallopian tubes, ovaries, uterus, cervix, and vagina.

Sex Organs

Sex organs are important parts of our bodies. Some people call them reproductive organs because they are involved in making and taking care of a fetus. As you grow, your sex organs grow and change, too. Some sex organs are inside your body, and others are outside. The ovaries, the fallopian tubes, and the uterus are primary reproductive organs that are inside your body. Breasts are examples of secondary reproductive organs.

The Ovaries

Women generally have two ovaries. Each one is about the size and shape of an almond. The job of the ovaries is to release eggs, or ova. All of the eggs a woman will ever have are already in her ovaries when she is born. During puberty, some of these eggs begin to ripen. A hormone made by the pituitary gland in the brain causes this ripening. Each month, the ovaries release one egg. This process is called ovulation.

The Fallopian Tubes

The fallopian tubes, not much thicker than strings of spaghetti, are on both sides of the top of the uterus. They have fringed ends like tiny fingers. Their function is to guide the ripened egg into the uterus.

The Uterus

One of the main sexual organs involved with PMS is the uterus, or womb. The uterus is shaped like an upside-down pear. Even in an adult female, it is only about the size of a fist. (Imagine a baby growing in there!) The uterus has muscular walls that expand during pregnancy.

The lower part or opening of the uterus is called the cervix. The cervix connects the uterus to the vaginal canal. The vagina acts as a passage to the outside of the body. When a woman has a menstrual period, blood flows from the uterus to the vagina and outside the body. (When a woman has a baby, the baby moves down this canal to be born.)

An egg's journey to the uterus begins when it is released from the ovary. Then it begins to move through the fallopian tube. If a woman has sexual intercourse during this time, sperm might join with the egg, and fertilization may take place. If it does, the fertilized egg travels to the uterus. After floating around in the uterus for a few days, the fertilized egg becomes implanted in the wall of the uterus and begins to develop and grow. At this time, pregnancy has begun.

The Menstrual Cycle

Every month, a woman's body prepares for fertilization and pregnancy. Obviously, most months fertilization and pregnancy do not occur. When they do not, the uterus discards its lining of blood and tissues that it has built up in preparation for pregnancy. This process is called menstruation. Hormones cause the monthly cycle, which is somewhat different in each woman.

It may seem as if you are losing a lot of blood with each period, or menstrual cycle, but the amount is usually not much. The usual discharge for a menstrual period is about four to six tablespoons, which your body quickly replaces.

One thing to remember is that there is no such thing as a "normal" period. Cycles can vary from twenty to thirty-six days, and periods can vary in length from two to seven days. Menstrual flow can be bright red or brownish. Your period may not be regular when it first starts in terms of how long it lasts or how long the cycle is, but in time it should become regular. If you become concerned about any aspect of your menstrual cycle, you always can talk to your doctor or health-care provider about it.

Your Cycle: The Sum of Its Parts

The first day of bleeding is considered the first day of your menstrual cycle. Although we know that cycles vary in length, twenty-eight days is the average.

The first half of the cycle is called the follicular phase or egg phase. The follicle is a bubble that surrounds each egg in the ovary. Various things happen in the follicular phase. First the uterus sheds its lining and causes several days of bleeding (your menstrual period). A hormone from the pituitary gland in the

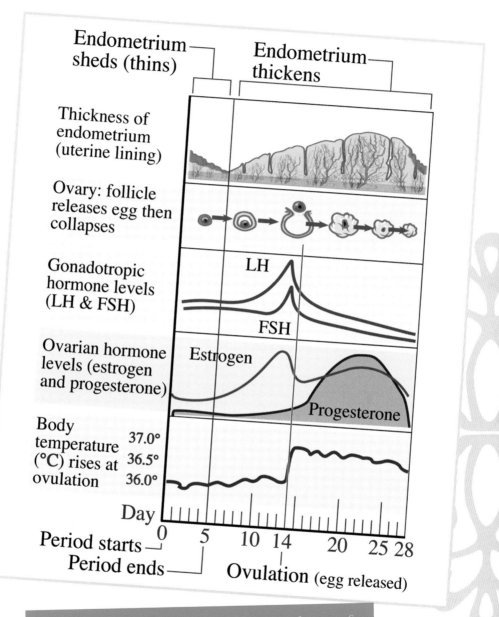

Endometrium sheds (thins)

Endometrium thickens

Thickness of endometrium (uterine lining)

Ovary: follicle releases egg then collapses

Gonadotropic hormone levels (LH & FSH)

LH

FSH

Ovarian hormone levels (estrogen and progesterone)

Estrogen

Progesterone

Body temperature (°C) rises at ovulation

37.0°
36.5°
36.0°

Day

0   5   10 14   20   25 28

Period starts

Period ends

Ovulation (egg released)

The above chart shows the different phases of a twenty-eight day menstrual cycle, as well as what happens in each phase and its duration.

brain makes an egg ripen. At the same time, the ovaries are making estrogen, a hormone that causes the lining of the uterus to thicken. On or about the fourteenth day of your cycle, the egg matures (becomes ripe) and bursts out of the ovary. This process is called ovulation. Some people can feel ovulation as a little twinge or pinch, but most women never notice it.

The second part of your cycle is called the luteal phase. This is the part of the cycle in which PMS may occur. After the egg is released, the bubble in which it was stored caves in. This caved-in area manufactures a second important hormone, progesterone. Progesterone makes the inside of the uterus even thicker. If the egg is not fertilized by a sperm, the uterus sheds its lining at this point. The first day of the next menstrual cycle (your period) begins.

2

The Symptoms of PMS

People who study premenstrual syndrome have discovered about 150 symptoms that may be experienced. Some women have only one of these symptoms each month. Other women have more.

Here is a list of the most common symptoms of PMS, divided into two groups, physical and emotional. It is possible for a person who has PMS to experience both physical and emotional symptoms.

Physical Symptoms of PMS

- Headache
- Back pain
- Abdominal bloating (swelling)
- Swelling of the hands and feet
- Tenderness and swelling of the breasts
- Pain in the joints

Acne is one of the most common physical symptoms of PMS. Many women find that they develop acne in the week before their period.

- Muscle stiffness
- Fatigue or inability to sleep
- Acne or rashes
- Cravings for salty or sweet foods, especially chocolate
- Dizziness
- Cold sores
- Discomfort in bright light
- Constipation

Emotional Symptoms of PMS

- Irritability
- Anger
- Hostility

- Depression
- Mood swings
- Loneliness
- Inability to concentrate
- Decreased or increased interest in sex
- Paranoia (the feeling that someone or something is out to get you)
- Tense relationships with family members and friends
- Strong desire to be alone

MYTH Premenstrual syndrome is all in your head.

FACT Despite the fact that experts are not completely sure what causes PMS, it is acknowledged as a very real condition. It needs to be treated seriously.

MYTH There is nothing you can do to alleviate PMS or cramps. You just have to live with it.

FACT Although there is no cure for PMS, there are ways to cope. To prevent swelling, bloating, or breast tenderness, steer clear of salt and caffeine for two weeks before your period. Reducing caffeine can

help alleviate anxiety, insomnia, and irritability as well. Schedule time for energizing exercise, and make sure to get enough sleep.

MYTH Exercise will make PMS symptoms worse.

FACT Exercise actually can ease PMS symptoms. The secret is to get into an exercise routine before symptoms start. Exercise all month, a little every day if possible. Exercise raises your level of beta-endorphins, the body's natural painkillers.

MYTH Diuretics are helpful for PMS because they decrease the bloated feeling.

FACT Diuretics are not good for you. They do remove water from the body, but they may leave you feeling sluggish. Also, they may deplete your supply of potassium, an important body chemical. Instead, cut back on salt, which can contribute to bloating.

MYTH If you suffer from only physical symptoms, you do not have PMS.

FACT Different people have different symptoms of PMS. Some women deal with physical symptoms. Others have more trouble with emotional changes. Some young women have a bit of each.

Cramps are often worst during the first day or two of your period. If you have painful cramps, ask your doctor about ways to ease the pain.

What PMS Is Not

PMS is not the same as dysmenorrhea, the painful cramps that may accompany a menstrual period. Usually the main symptom of painful menstruation is cramping in the pelvic area (lower abdomen). Cramps start about the same time as your period and can continue for a few days. Along with cramping, you may have nausea, vomiting, back pain, dizziness, tiredness, or bloating.

In the teenage years, dysmenorrhea is more common than PMS. One theory is that the uterine muscles tighten to push out the menstrual blood, and this tightening may cause the dysmenorrhea. In addition, the uterus makes some chemicals of its own, called prostaglandins. Some researchers think women have menstrual cramps because their prostaglandins are out of balance.

3

Recognizing PMS

No one knows exactly what causes PMS. One possible cause is a change in hormone levels that occurs before menstruation. Hormones are chemical substances made by glands in your body. The hormones that are most important in the menstrual cycle are estrogen and progesterone.

Although all women experience a change in hormone levels before menstruation, not all women have PMS or menstrual discomfort. Why does one young woman have PMS while another does not? According to one theory, the cause of PMS is low progesterone levels in the second half of the menstrual cycle. Some experts believe that female hormones act in combination with brain chemicals to cause PMS. Most doctors consider a person's whole "self"—her social life, family life, school life, and personal life—before making a diagnosis of PMS. Though the condition is hard to diagnose, it's estimated that about three-quarters of all women experience PMS.

Getting Help

If you have problems with your menstrual cycle or have questions about PMS, you should see a physician or another health-care provider. The best time to see a doctor about premenstrual symptoms is when you are not having them. At that time, you will be calmer and can give a better description of your symptoms.

You may choose to see your regular doctor, or you may want to go to a clinic that specializes in treating teenage patients (an adolescent clinic). Another option is to see a gynecologist. A gynecologist is a doctor who specializes in treating conditions of the female

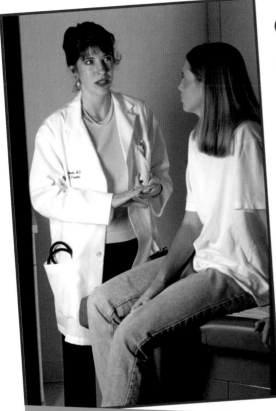

If your primary care physician does not deal with reproductive health issues or menstrual problems, she or he will be able to help you find someone who does.

reproductive system. Some young women prefer to see a female gynecologist. Whether you choose a male or female doctor, be assured that gynecologists are trained professionals who are sensitive to your concerns. If they are not, you have a right to request another provider or request a second opinion.

What Will the Doctor Want to Know?

The doctor probably will ask some of the following questions:

- Why do you believe you may have PMS? What are your symptoms? Do they always occur before your period?
- How long is your usual menstrual period, and how much time is there between periods?
- How old were you when you first started to menstruate?
- What's going on with your life, your school, your family, and your friends?
- What effect do you think PMS might be having on your self-esteem, your friendships, and your other relationships?
- Have you had any previous help with your problem? What has worked? What has not worked?

Your PMS Calendar

The only way most women can remember what happens with their menstrual and premenstrual symptoms and when they occur is to keep a diary or chart. A simple way to keep track is to note your symptoms on your own PMS calendar. You will be most likely to write on your calendar when you are feeling badly and have symptoms. But try writing something on the days you feel good, too.

Here are some guidelines for keeping a
PMS calendar:

- Weigh yourself every morning when you get up. Weigh without clothes and after you go to the bathroom. Do

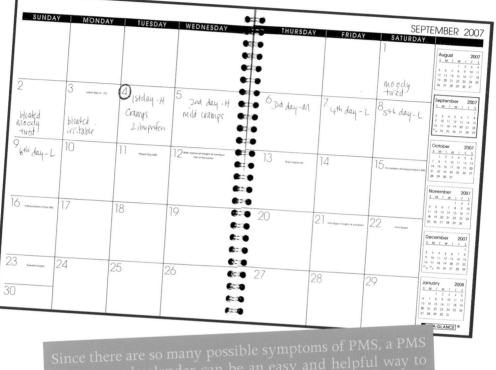

Since there are so many possible symptoms of PMS, a PMS or menstrual calendar can be an easy and helpful way to keep track of your physical and emotional symptoms.

the same things in the same order every day, and record your weight.

• Write down the physical and emotional symptoms that you experience.

• Give the strength of your symptoms a rating: 1 = mild; 2 = medium; 3 = severe.

• Write down any medications you currently are taking and their dosage.

• Write down any major dietary changes, food cravings, or food binges when they occur.

10 Great Questions to Ask Your Doctor About PMS

1. How do you diagnose premenstrual syndrome (PMS)?

2. Could my PMS symptoms be those of another medical condition?

3. What over-the-counter medication, if any, would you recommend?

4. What can I do to alleviate PMS symptoms?

5. Are there certain foods I should eat more of or foods I should avoid to help alleviate PMS symptoms?

6. Are certain types of exercise better than others? How much exercise should I get?

7. As I get older, will my PMS symptoms get better, get worse, or stay the same?

8. Would you recommend any vitamin or mineral supplements?

9. Under what conditions would you recommend prescription medication?

10. Is there any way I can prevent PMS from occurring?

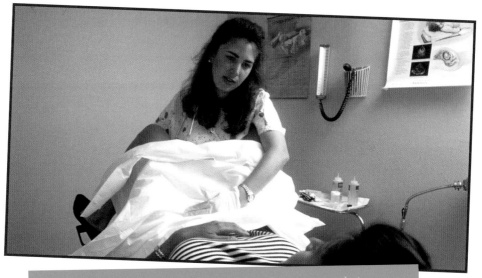

If you have questions or concerns during a pelvic exam, you should feel free to bring them up with your doctor at any time during the procedure.

The Gynecological Exam

Your doctor will not be able to diagnose PMS from an exam or through laboratory tests, and he or she might recommend that you see a gynecologist to make sure that your symptoms are not the result of another medical condition. Other conditions, such as depression, anemia, thyroid disorders, and diabetes, need to be ruled out before a diagnosis of PMS can be made.

The doctor will want to ask you questions about your symptoms and conduct a pelvic exam. You will be asked to put on a hospital gown or just take off your pants and underwear. Next you will sit or lie down on an examining table. Although it is very common to be embarrassed, remember that examining you is the doctor's job, and your health is the primary concern.

The doctor will ask you to put your feet in metal holders called stirrups. The doctor will examine the outside parts of your genital organs. Then he or she will insert a gloved finger into the vagina to feel the cervix (the lower part of the uterus). Though it is rare, sometimes he or she also will insert a finger into the rectum to get an idea of the size and position of the uterus. Another part of the exam is the insertion into the vagina of an instrument called a speculum. The speculum gently spreads open the vagina so that the doctor can see your cervix. Although parts of the exam may be uncomfortable and you may feel pressure, you should not feel any pain. If you do, tell the doctor. The doctor or health-care provider should explain exactly what he or she is doing at all times. If he or she is not communicating with you, ask him or her to explain.

4

Treatment and Relief

A lot of people are confused regarding the treatment for premenstrual symptoms. That might be because what works for one woman might not work for another. It is important to find what works for you.

Some treatments for PMS are trial and error. When trying out a treatment, be sure to use common sense. A general rule is to use moderation (not too much and not too little) in your treatment. Many of the following tips are simply common-sense advice for healthy living. They should help your PMS. They also will make you a healthier person and help you feel in control of your life.

Some suggestions may not help your PMS. That's OK. Use the ideas that work, and never mind about the others. Be sure to give whatever you try time to work. Some treatments for PMS may work well one month but not the next month. Keep a record for several months, and then decide.

One tip: some of the remedies will work both for PMS and for painful menstruation.

Old and New Treatments

Years ago (maybe in your mother's or grandmother's generation), hot baths and heating pads were the only remedies for menstrual pain. We have many more remedies today, but let's not ignore those that work. If a warm bath helps your discomfort, fill up the tub and take a soak. If a heating pad makes you feel better, plug it in and turn it on. These days, however, we have additional treatments for PMS.

Lifestyle Remedies

Lifestyle remedies involve changing the way you live. A healthy lifestyle offers all sorts of physical and emotional benefits. Proper nutrition, exercise, and a balanced lifestyle can alleviate PMS symptoms and help you to better cope with the condition. Here are some tips for changing your lifestyle for the better.

Healthful Eating and Drinking Habits

One of the most important lifestyle changes you can make is to start eating in a healthy way. Follow these dietary dos and don'ts all the time to make you more comfortable all month long.

- Do eat frequent small meals, rather than a few big ones. This will keep your system from getting overloaded at any one time. Frequent small meals keep your energy level up.

A healthy diet can help PMS symptoms. Eat complex carbohydrates that are high in fiber. Cut back on sugar, fats, and caffeine. Avoid foods that have a lot of salt. Drink plenty of water to stay hydrated.

- Do eat lots of whole-grain products, such as cereals made with wheat, corn, oats, and other grains. Popcorn (without a lot of oil and butter) makes a great snack food.
- Do eat at least five servings a day of fresh fruits and vegetables. Green, red, and orange vegetables like broccoli, lettuce, tomatoes, and carrots are super. They are packed with vitamins and are low in calories. Almost any vegetable you can think of is good.
- Do try to increase your intake of calcium, since calcium seems to relieve cramping. Foods that increase calcium without adding lots of calories are skim milk, low-fat yogurt, broccoli, kale, and collard greens.
- Do try to increase your intake of magnesium. Magnesium seems to help reduce breast tenderness, water retention and bloating, and mood swings. Foods containing magnesium include broccoli, spinach, yogurt, whole-grain cereals, nuts, and seafood.
- Don't drink beverages containing caffeine. If you're tired and need a lift, taking a nap would be better. Caffeine may lift you up for a little while or give you a "buzz," but it lets you down later. Caffeine can lead to anxiety and irritability. It may increase breast tenderness. Avoid coffee, tea, cola, and chocolate. It's better to drink water (plain or with lemon) or herbal tea.
- Don't let too many sweet things cross your lips. Sugar has an effect similar to caffeine: it picks you up, then lets you down. As a result, you're more tired than before. Artificial sweeteners don't solve the problem. The body reacts to them as if they were sugar.

- Don't overdo on salt. Salt helps hold water in the body and may lead to bloating. Remember that a lot of sodium (salt) is used in canned foods, such as soups and vegetables. In other words, it's already there and we don't even notice it.
- Don't take vitamin pills in high doses. This can be dangerous.

Exercise

Some people think exercise makes their PMS symptoms worse. The secret is to get into a routine before symptoms start. Exercise all month, a little every day if possible. Such activity raises your level of beta-endorphins, the body's natural painkillers. Try one or more of the following for about thirty minutes a day to increase your feeling of well-being.

- **Walking.** This is a great way to start your exercise program. You can walk somewhere, such as to a friend's house, or you and a friend can go walking for the fun and fitness of it. (Include your dog, and you'll have another friend.)
- **Jogging.** This works up more of a sweat than walking and is a fast way to burn up calories and exercise your entire body.
- **Swimming.** Of course, swimming requires access to a pool, but doing your laps won't make you sweat—or at least you won't notice it. Swimming for a minimum of twenty minutes a day will relax your muscles as well as your mind.

- **Biking.** You can bicycle outdoors while watching
  the scenery, or you can use a stationary bike inside
  and combine your exercise with reading or listening
  to music.

All of the above are forms of aerobic exercise. Any exercise
that gets oxygen to your muscles is aerobic. Other kinds include
dancing and aerobics classes.

Try to get some form of exercise every day. If that's impossible,
try for three times a week. If it's not too far, walk to school
instead of taking the bus or driving. Write what you did on
your personal calendar or in your journal. Give yourself credit
for moving around!

Stress Reduction

A third lifestyle change is to reduce your stress. No one can ever
get rid of all stress in his or her life. In fact, we wouldn't want to
eliminate it. Without some stress, life would be boring. Deadlines,
for example, help us get things done. However, sometimes we
have too many deadlines—and too much stress.

The first step in reducing stress is to recognize that it's there.
Then take steps to get rid of it little by little. Take a look at your
life. Do you have to be class secretary, a member of the debate team,
editor of the newspaper, a basketball player, a Sunday school
teacher, and a babysitter? Could you drop one of these activities?
Remember, you don't have to hold up the world all by yourself.

You can try the following techniques for stress relief:

- **Refocus.** Realize that you are responsible for yourself
  and for yourself only. You cannot change your mother,

your father, your sister, your boyfriend, or your girl-friend. Letting go of the wish to change others should take your stress level down a notch or two.

- **Relax.** Let go of body tension. One way is to put on headphones and listen to peaceful music. Another way is to close your eyes and imagine a peaceful time and place. The seashore? The mountains? Yourself as a baby? Still another method of relaxing is to lie on your back and concentrate on one part of your body at a time. Start with your scalp. Feel it relax. Then move to your eyes. Let your eyelids get heavy and tired. Then feel your jaw muscles. Are they tight? Let them relax. Keep moving down your body, relaxing one part at a time until you get to your toes. By this time, you should feel relaxed all over.

- **Meditate.** Meditation is a way of blocking out trouble-some thoughts and giving your mind a rest. Meditating can take many forms. Here is one simple way: Sit or lie down in a comfortable position. Close your eyes. Take slow, deep breaths. Concentrate on your breathing. Keep out all other thoughts. As you inhale, count 1–2–3 slowly. As you exhale, count 1–2–3 again. Keep doing this as long as you can. Try for five minutes at a stretch.

- **Use affirmations.** Affirmations are positive things you say about yourself to yourself. Think up some affirmations about PMS, and say each one at least three times. Here are some examples: "I can manage premenstrual syndrome." "I am trying to eat and sleep well." "My relationships with people are good and satisfying."

Yoga can increase flexibility and tone muscles as well as reduce stress. Once you learn proper yoga techniques, you can practice almost anywhere.

- **Do yoga.** The best way to learn yoga is to take a class. These breathing and stretching exercises can help reduce stress, but it's important to learn to do yoga correctly.
- **Get a massage.** Massage is a way of touching that soothes and relaxes muscles and relieves stress. Some massage even relieves headaches. You can take classes on how to give and receive massages. Or you can go to a certified massage therapist.
- **Be creative.** Using your creative abilities can relieve stress. The possibilities are endless: Try baking, drawing, painting, writing, working with clay, gardening, jewelry-making, knitting, playing or writing music, singing, or any other activity that you enjoy.

Getting enough sleep is important. Teenagers need about nine hours of sleep a night. In addition, try to maintain a regular schedule of meals, exercise, and bedtime.

- **Write in a journal.** Journal writing is a chore for some people, but for others it provides release from stress. Record observations about yourself and your relationships, emotions, diet, exercise, stresses, stress relievers, goals, and dreams.

Sleep

The fourth lifestyle remedy is getting enough sleep. Before going to sleep, clear your mind of troublesome thoughts. Use a stress-relief method, such as meditation, soft music, or a cup of warm milk. Some people feel great after a fifteen-minute nap. Others feel groggy and would rather sleep only at night.

Humor

Finally, laugh! Humor is a good remedy for any problem. See a funny play or movie, or read the comics or a humorous book. Instead of growling at people, remind yourself that PMS is not a fatal disease. It is an inconvenience you share with many other women.

Psychotherapy

Psychotherapy involves changing the way you think and feel. It can help sort out thoughts and feelings. PMS may make you feel as if you are losing control. Or during your premenstrual phase, you may feel down on yourself. You may feel irritable, angry, or sad. Remember that PMS is very common, and most people don't need to seek therapy to deal with it. If PMS comes with severe emotional stresses, or it makes those issues more difficult to deal with, you then may want to try therapy.

There are several ways to get support with tangled emotions: self-help, individual or group psychotherapy, and support groups.

Self-Help

If you are reading this, you are taking the most important step—helping yourself. You are taking responsibility for yourself, your body, and your emotions. This self-help will be useful to you for your whole life. Self-help does not mean acting as your own doctor. It means believing in yourself as a competent person with a medical problem, PMS.

If PMS hurts your self-esteem, you might want to try these exercises. They will help strengthen your self-image. Make a list

If you are experiencing low self-esteem as a result of PMS, take some time to write down your strengths, talents, and accomplishments. Focusing on these positives can make you feel happier and more self-confident.

of all your good qualities. What do you like about yourself? What do other people like about you? Are you ever your own worst enemy? When and under what circumstances? Write down the qualities in yourself that you would like to change. When you talk to yourself, do you say good things or negative things? What are your goals for yourself? Are they within your reach? For example, is it realistic to say you're going to exercise two hours every day? Why not start with thirty minutes every other day?

Individual or Group Therapy and Support Groups

Self-help exercises are useful, but you may need extra support from a counselor like a social worker or psychologist. The person who counsels you must understand that PMS is not "all in your mind." If you are currently seeing a therapist, make sure he or she understands premenstrual syndrome. Support groups offer a means by which you can meet and talk with people who are experiencing similar problems or symptoms. If you need help finding a therapist or support group, talk to you doctor, school nurse, or school counselor. Getting emotional support and knowing you are not alone can go a long way in helping you cope with PMS.

Medications

Sometimes lifestyle changes or changing the way you think are not enough. At this point, you may want to look into medications. One choice is to try over-the-counter (nonprescription) medications, or you can ask the doctor for a prescription.

The most commonly prescribed medication for the relief of discomfort caused by PMS is ibuprofen. Ibuprofen also is sold

If your symptoms do not improve with nutrition or lifestyle changes, talk to your doctor about medications that might help. Ibuprofen or naproxen (such as Aleve) can help relieve lower back pain, cramps, and headaches.

over the counter under various trade names, such as Advil, Nuprin, and Motrin. Ibuprofen seems to stop the buildup of prostaglandins. These are the substances that the body produces in the second half of the menstrual cycle.

Before you use this or any other medication, read the instructions on the label and packaging. Knowing how and when to take any drug will help you get the best results and avoid bad side effects.

Your doctor may prescribe another anti-inflammatory drug, such as naproxen (Anaprox or Naprosyn). Naproxen also is available over-the-counter under the trade name Aleve. Other over-the-counter pain relievers are acetaminophen (like Tylenol) and aspirin. See what works best for you. Remember, if there is any chance you might be pregnant, avoid all drugs.

Some physicians prescribe low-dose birth control pills for PMS. These seem to even out the hormonal changes that may be one cause of the problem. For some people, however, birth control pills make PMS worse. Pay careful attention to your body signals, and keep notes in your journal or on your PMS calendar.

Unproven Remedies

Many women use various vitamins and minerals to help with PMS. Some take vitamin B6 or multiple B vitamins. Others take vitamin E. Some people take zinc, magnesium, or calcium pills. Oil of evening primrose, a plant oil available in health food stores, is another popular preparation. However, even if you choose to use vitamins, minerals, or other alternative treatments, be sure to let your doctor know. All of the remedies mentioned here are unproven.

Things to Avoid

If possible, do not use the following remedies:

- Antidepressants and tranquilizers. Doctors often prescribe these medications for depression (low moods). But antidepressants take two weeks to build up an effect, so they have limited usefulness in PMS.
- Diuretics, sometimes called water pills. They remove water from the body, but they may leave you feeling sluggish. Also, they may deplete your supply of potassium, an important body chemical.

5

A Few Final Words

Sometimes premenstrual syndrome is mistaken for other medical conditions. If you have serious symptoms, it's important to go to a doctor. Two medical conditions are sometimes confused with PMS. The first is endometriosis, a condition in which tissue related to the lining of the uterus spreads outside the uterus. A woman with endometriosis may have pain before her period and severe cramps during her period. The second is pelvic inflammatory disease (PID), an infection that affects the lining of the uterus, fallopian tubes, and/or ovaries. In PID, the pain is constant. In PMS, the pain usually goes away soon after menstruation starts.

The Plus Side

Some women actually feel better before their periods. They are more energetic and more creative. Being creative means putting some of yourself into producing something new and different.

The Internet can be an extremely helpful resource when learning about PMS. Just for starters, you can find articles about going to the gynecologist, getting your period, and food and fitness tips.

Some say creativity comes from suffering. Maybe the discomfort experienced by women with PMS helps them become more creative people.

For some, the premenstrual phase is a chance to let go of the tight control they may keep themselves under most of the time. However, PMS should never be used as an excuse for behavior that is inappropriate.

PMS Resources

Often young women with PMS feel as if no one understands them. They don't know where to turn for education, advice, and support.

If you reach out, there are many places to get support. Your doctor, family, and friends can be great sources of support. There may be community organizations or support groups in your area. Most large cities have adolescent clinics and gynecological offices. If you do not have access to resources like these, you might want to do some research. There are probably books on PMS at your local library that you can check out for more information. The Internet also can be a great place to research and get support for PMS.

Remember that treatment for PMS is individualized. What works for one woman may not work for another. You have to keep trying different things. PMS may be stubborn, but it can be alleviated. Some of the healing will come with the help of education and support from friends and professionals, such as doctors and counselors. The rest of the healing will come from you.

Glossary

beta-endorphins Chemical substances in the blood that may influence pain.

bloated Having body tissues filled with fluid.

cervix Opening to the uterus.

diuretic Medication that causes the body to get rid of water.

dysmenorrhea Painful menstruation.

endometriosis Condition in which tissue related to the lining of the uterus spreads to other parts of the body.

estrogen A female hormone.

fallopian tubes Tubes on each side of the uterus in which conception usually takes place.

fertilization The joining of a sperm with an egg, creating a fetus.

gynecologist A doctor who specializes in diseases and conditions of the female reproductive system.

hormones Chemical substances secreted by special glands that influence body functioning.

menstruation Female monthly bleeding; also called a period.

ovaries Female organs that produce eggs (ova).

ovulation The release of an egg from the ovary.

progesterone A female hormone.

prostaglandins Hormones that help the uterus tighten and contract.

puberty The period of rapid physical change in both males and females that usually occurs in the teen years.

speculum An instrument used in gynecological examinations.

uterus Womb; pear-shaped organ in which a baby develops.

For More Information

American College of Obstetricians and Gynecologists (ACOG)
409 12th Street SW
P.O. Box 96920
Washington, DC 20090-6920
(202) 638-5577
Web site: http://ww.acog.org

> The American College of Obstetricians and Gynecologists offers fact sheets and resources on women's health topics.

Center for Young Women's Health
Children's Hospital Boston
333 Longwood Avenue, 5th Floor
Boston, MA 02115
(617) 355-2994
Web site: http://www.youngwomenshealth.org

> This center's Web site offers information on various health topics and has sections on menstruation, PMS, and cramps.

Planned Parenthood Federation of America
434 West 33rd Street
New York, NY 10001
(212) 541-7800
Web site: http://www.plannedparenthood.org

> Planned Parenthood provides sexual and reproductive health care and education. Its Web site offers information about birth control, STDs, and referrals to local clinics.

U.S. Department of Health and Human Services
Office on Women's Health
200 Independence Avenue SW, Room 712E
Washington, DC 20201
(202) 690-7650
Web site: www.4woman.gov/faq/pms.htm

> This government agency was established in 1991 to coordinate the efforts of the Health and Human Services agencies involved in women's health. Its mission is to work toward improving the health and well-being of women and girls in the United States.

Web Sites

Due to the changing nature of Internet links, Rosen Publishing has developed an online list of Web sites related to the subject of this book. This site is updated regularly. Please use this link to access the list:

http://www.rosenlinks.com/gh/dpms

For Further Reading

Boston Women's Health Book Collective. *Our Bodies, Ourselves: A New Edition for a New Era*. New York, NY: Touchstone, 2005.

Gregson, Susan R. *Premenstrual Syndrome* (Perspectives on Physical Health). Mankato, MN: LifeMatters, 2000.

Loulan, JoAnn, and Bonnie Worthen. *Period. A Girl's Guide*. Minnetonka, MN: Book Peddlers, 2001.

Madaras, Lynda. *The "What's Happening to My Body?" Book for Girls: A Growing-Up Guide for Parents and Daughters*. New York, NY: Newmarket Press, 2000.

Mason, Mary-Claire. *Coping Successfully with Period Problems* (Overcoming Common Problems). London, England: Sheldon Press, 2006.

Moe, Barbara. *Coping with PMS*. New York, NY: Rosen Publishing, 2001.

Taylor, Nadine. *25 Natural Ways to Relieve PMS*. New York, NY: McGraw-Hill, 2002.

Bibliography

Boston Women's Health Book Collective. *Our Bodies, Ourselves: A New Edition for a New Era*. New York, NY: Touchstone, 2005.

Britannica Online. "Human Reproductive System." Retrieved August 2006 (http://www.search.eb.com/eb/article-9110811).

Britannica Online. "Premenstrual Syndrome." Retrieved August 2006 (http://www.search.eb.com/eb/article-9061261).

Dalton, Katharina. *Once a Month: Understanding and Treating PMS*. Alameda, CA: Hunter House Publishers, 1999.

Lark, Susan. *Premenstrual Syndrome Self-Help Book*. Berkeley, CA: Celestial Arts, 1989.

Manassiev, Nikolai, and Malcolm I. Whitehead, eds. *Female Reproductive Health*. Abingdon, UK: Taylor & Francis, 2003.

WebMD. "Sexual Health: Your Guide to Premenstrual Syndrome." Retrieved August 2006 (http://www.webmd.com/content/article/10/2953_497.htm).

WomensHealth.gov. "Menstruation and the Menstrual Cycle." Retrieved August 2006 (http://www.womenshealth.gov/faq/menstru.htm).

WomensHealth.gov. "Premenstrual Syndrome." Retrieved August 2006 (http://www.womenshealth.gov/faq/pms.htm).

Index

A
acne, 14
antidepressants, 38

B
backaches, 4, 13, 17
birth control pills, for PMS relief, 38
bloating, 4, 13, 15, 16, 17, 28
breasts, 6, 8, 13, 15, 28

C
caffeine, avoiding, 15–16, 28
cervix, 9, 24
cramps, 15, 17, 28, 39

D
diuretics, 16, 38
dysmenorrhea, 17

E
eating habits, healthy, 26–29
emotions, 5, 7, 13, 14–15, 16, 26,
    28, 34
endometriosis, 39
estrogen, 12, 18
exercise, 16, 22, 29–30

F
fallopian tubes, 8, 9, 39

F
fatigue/tiredness, 14, 17
food cravings, 4, 14

G
gynecologist, 19, 23–24

H
headaches, 4, 13, 32
hormones, 7–9, 12, 18, 38

I
ibuprofen, 36–37

L
lifestyle remedies for PMS, 26–34

M
menstruation
    cycle of, 10–12
    defined/described, 9, 10
    hormones and, 8

N
naproxen, 37

O
ovaries, 8–9, 10, 39
ovulation, 9, 12

Photo Credits

Cover, pp. 3, 4 © www.istockphoto.com/Justin Horrocks; cover (inset photos), pp. 1, 4 and 5 (inset photos), 22 Shutterstock.com and © www.istockphoto.com/Ravet007; p. 7 © Cleo Photography/Photo Edit; p. 8 © www.istockphoto.com/Dawn Johnston; p. 11 © 2007 Nucleus Medical Art, All rights reserved. www.nucleusinc.com; p. 14 © Bannor/Custom Medical Stock Photo; p. 17 © Mary Kay Denny/Photo Edit; p. 19 © Will & Deni McIntyre/Photo Researchers, Inc.; p. 23 © Michael Newman/Photo Edit; pp. 27, 40 Shutterstock.com; p. 32 © www.istockphoto.com/Alexander Katina; p. 33 © www.istockphoto.com/Tyler Stalman; p. 35 © www.istockphoto.com/Ana Blazic, p. 37 © Getty Images.

Designer: Evelyn Horovicz; **Photo Research:** Cindy Reiman